Whose Birthday Is It Anyway?

A Children's Christmas Program

Phyllis Maclay

CSS Publishing Company, Inc., Lima, Ohio

WHOSE BIRTHDAY IS IT ANYWAY?

Reprinted 2002

Copyright © 1997 by
CSS Publishing Company, Inc.
Lima, Ohio

For more information about CSS Publishing Company resources, visit our website at www.csspub.com or e-mail us at custserv@csspub.com or call (800) 241-4056.

ISBN 0-7880-1055-7   PRINTED IN U.S.A.

To Mrs. Innes, who got me started,
Jennie Todd, who kept me going,
And Mom, who has always supported me.

Order Of Worship

Call To Worship

Opening Hymn: "There's A Song In The Air"

Scripture: Luke 2:1-20

Hymn: "Away In A Manger"

Prayer

Hymn: "Joy To The World"

Offering

Doxology

Responsive Reading

Hymn: "Angels We Have Heard On High"

Play: Whose Birthday Is It Anyway?

Benediction

Production Note

The animals in Act 2 may wear costumes to identify them. Women in the church could be asked to volunteer to make the donkey and dove costumes from patterns that are available. The sheep can wear solid black or white sweatpants and sweatshirts with contrasting knee socks on their arms and legs. Sweatbands with ears attached will complete the proper effect. The doves can wear white sweatpants and sweatshirts with tissue paper folded accordion style and pinned on the back as wings and tail feathers. The song "The Friendly Beasts" can be found in many church hymnals. It is also available as sheet music in most music stores.

Whose Birthday Is It Anyway?

Cast

Angel	Three Doves
Boy	Four Cows
Two Donkeys	Four Sheep

Act 1

(A group of youth cross over, talking of Christmas lists, mostly of what they are getting. A group of adults crosses over, discussing the same, mostly of what they are giving, carrying shopping bags full of presents. A young boy watches, appearing troubled at what he hears. He walks center stage, as an angel hovers in the background.)

Boy: *(Shakes his head)* Just listen to them. It's all anybody talks about. Shopping, shopping, shopping! It's okay at first. But now it's making my parents cranky. And it's all my sister talks about. "I want, I want, I want." It just doesn't seem right.

Angel: And why not?

Boy: *(Looks startled, but continues talking)* Well, whose birthday is it anyway? When it's MY birthday, I get the gifts. Christmas is Jesus' birthday. What does HE get?

7

Angel: Very little attention, I'm afraid.

Boy: It makes me wonder —

Angel: How did it get this way?

Boy: Yeah.

Angel: And why do we get so involved with the commercial side of Christmas that we forget its true meaning?

Boy: Yeah, that's it. Was it always this way?

Angel: Oh, no. I remember a very special Christmas.

Boy: Who are you, anyway?

Angel: I'm an angel.

Boy: Yeah, right. And I'm Barney.

Angel: *(Laughing)* Don't you believe in angels?

Boy: Yeah, but, you don't look like one.

Angel: Don't tell me — you were expecting wings!

Boy: Well —

Angel: And a long white robe and halo?

Boy: Uh, well ...

Angel: Come on, it's 199_ *(present year)*. But if it makes you more comfortable, I'll humor you with a halo *(puts one on)*. Better?

Boy: Wow, you really are an angel. But why are you here?

Angel: To show you something. To let you know Christmas wasn't always like this. One very special Christmas, long ago, JESUS was the center of attention. Why, even the friendly beasts bestowed him with blessed tokens of love and adoration. That's angel talk for birthday presents.

Boy: I knew that.

Angel: Just come with me for a few moments, and I'll show you ... *(They exit together)*

Act 2

(Beasts come in singing first verse of "The Friendly Beasts." Mary and Joseph enter carrying baby, go to side after song.)

Cow 1: I can't believe it! The Son of God was born right here in our stable. Wait until I tell the cows in the back pasture what they missed tonight!

Donkey 1: Mary and Joseph look so tired.

Donkey 2: No wonder! It was a long ride to Bethlehem. My achin' hooves still hurt.

Donkey 1: The roads were rough and rocky.

Donkey 2: But we made it! And just in time.

(All animals sing second verse of "The Friendly Beasts.")

Cow 2: Did you hear what his name is?

Cow 3: Yes. His name is JESUS.

Cow 4: Poor little thing. He needs a place to sleep. What should we do?

Cow 1: Cows, come here. Let's mo-o-o-ve out of the way and offer our manger.

Cow 4: What a good idea! The hay will be soft and warm.

(Cows step back. All animals sing third verse of "The Friendly Beasts." Mary and Joseph put Jesus in the manger.)

Sheep 1: It's getting cold in here.

Sheep 2: Poor Baby Jesus is shivering.

Sheep 3: We need to do something! What can we give him? We're only sheep.

Sheep 4: I've got it! We sheep can make a blanket for him from our wool.

Sheep 1: Here, take mine.

Sheep 2: Mine, too. It's really soft.

Sheep 3: Won't we get cold?

Sheep 4: We'll be all right. We must take care of Jesus first.

(All animals sing fourth verse of "The Friendly Beasts" as Mary finds blanket and covers baby. Mary and Joseph lie down.)

Dove 1: Now he's warm in his manger bed.

Dove 2: But why is he so squirmy? Oh, no! I think he's going to cry!

Dove 1: Mary and Joseph are asleep. They need their rest after their long journey and the baby's birth.

Dove 3: Baby Jesus feels all alone.

Dove 2: I know what we doves can do! We'll coo very softly until he falls asleep. Come, doves!

Dove 3: Hurry, before he cries!

(All the animals sing fifth verse of "The Friendly Beasts.")

Donkey 2: I'm glad we could see to it that they got here safely.

Cow 4: And we could give him a cozy place to sleep.

Sheep 4: And a warm blanket.

Dove 3: And a soft lullaby.

(All animals sing the last verse of "The Friendly Beasts.")

Act 3

(Angel and Boy come center stage)

Angel: So what did you learn from the friendly beasts?

Boy: That it's Jesus' birthday and we all have something to give him.

11

Angel: Even today?

Boy: Yes, especially today. There's something we all can give him. We just have to figure out what that is.

Angel: I couldn't have said it better myself.

Boy: We must always remember whose birthday it is when we celebrate Christmas. *(Turns to congregation)* And what will YOU give him this Christmas?

(Children sing "Happy Birthday To Jesus" as the cakes* are brought in. The Angel explains to the congregation that the children have made ornaments** for each person to take home and write on them their "gift" to Jesus. Give examples — drive neighbor to doctor, attend choir this year, help with scouting program, visit elderly, study more for tests in school, and so forth. Children serve cake to the congregation as members take home a Christmas ornament to remind them of their gift to Jesus. Congregation can either come forward and be served or remain seated as children serve them at their pews.)

The End

*Angel food cake baked in loaf pans and cut into bite-sized pieces.

** Ornaments can be made of paper, decorated simply, with a hole punched in them and string threaded through. Allow space for each person to write on them their "gift" to Jesus.